PENGUIN BOOKS

THE PENGUIN
BARBECUE
COOKBOOK

Over 100 recipes for great barbecues

THE PENGUIN
BARBECUE
COOKBOOK

Over 100 recipes for great barbecues

Syd Pemberton

PENGUIN BOOKS

Penguin Books

Published by the Penguin Group
Penguin Books Australia Ltd
250 Camberwell Road, Camberwell, Victoria 3124, Australia
Penguin Books Ltd
80 Strand, London WC2R 0RL, England
Penguin Putnam Inc.
375 Hudson Street, New York, New York 10014, USA
Penguin Books, a division of Pearson Canada
10 Alcorn Avenue, Toronto, Ontario, Canada M4V 3B2
Penguin Books (NZ) Ltd
Cnr Rosedale and Airborne Roads, Albany, Auckland, New Zealand
Penguin Books (South Africa) (Pty) Ltd
24 Sturdee Avenue, Rosebank, Johannesburg 2196, South Africa
Penguin Books India (P) Ltd
11, Community Centre, Panchsheel Park, New Delhi 110 017, India

First published by Penguin Books Australia Ltd 2003

10 9 8 7 6 5 4 3 2 1

Design by Brad Maxwell, Penguin Design Studio
Photographs by Julie Anne Renouf
Inside cover images © photolibrary.com
Typeset in NimbusSanNovTMed 9/11pt by Midland Typesetters, Maryborough, Victoria
Printed and bound in Australia by McPherson's Printing Group, Maryborough, Victoria

National Library of Australia
Cataloguing-in-Publication data:

Pemberton, Syd.
The Penguin barbecue cookbook.

Includes index.
ISBN 0 14 100807 5.

1. Barbecue cookery. I. Title.

641.5784

www.penguin.com.au

Contents

Introduction

When the sun is out and the weather is calm, there is nothing more satisfying than firing up the barbecue and cooking outdoors. Humans first cooked on an open fire thousands of years ago, and even today in some parts of the world this is the only method of cooking that people use. (Smoking food – especially salted meat – over a fire was a way of preserving it before any reliable method of refrigeration existed.)

In Australia, the barbecue is the most common form of get-together. The first real barbecue I cooked on was one my family built in our garden in England. We would stand huddled under an umbrella, watching the food cook over the hot coals on a cool, rainy summer's day. In Australia, I have enjoyed barbecuing out in the bush and in my own back garden, and even when it has rained here I have barbecued inside on a large cast-iron chargrill pan. This cooks food in the manner of a barbecue but it is not quite the same as outdoor cooking. Somehow the essence of the food is different and that special barbecue flavour is missing.

There are lots of types of barbecues but the art of a good barbecue is starting a fire and getting the coals just right, or preheating a gas barbecue to the correct temperature before cooking the food. Barbecuing is a simple cooking method that everyone can enjoy and all can share. There is nothing more fun than hanging around the barbecue, with tongs in hand, watching the food cooking away and inhaling the delicious barbecue aromas, with family or friends.

The recipes in this book are a selection of easy dishes that can feed the family or make an elegant lunch or dinner. Simplicity of ingredients with an interesting marinade, side dish or sauce can make a barbecued piece of food a taste sensation, causing everyone to come back for more – I know my family and friends did!

Barbecue tricks and tips

Before you start cooking, make sure you have all the equipment you need to hand, including tools for cooking, food at the right temperature to go straight onto the barbecue, and any condiments or marinades to brush over the food. If things only take a minute or two to cook, you don't want to be running into the house to get the tongs and then overcooking the food!

Remember not to leave raw food out in the sun, and clean any platters that have had raw food on them before re-use. It is a good idea to use two platters during the barbecuing process: one for taking the raw foods from, and the other for putting the cooked food onto.

Charcoal or wood-fired barbecues

Set the fire first, using either firelighters or small rolled-up knots of clean newspaper, and kindling wood. Make a layer of charcoal on the bottom then add a few firelighters or knots of newspaper, then cover with more charcoal. Once it gets going and there is a good fire, add some wood or some more charcoal.

R A wood fire will take about 30–45 minutes to produce suitable coals for cooking.

⋔ A charcoal fire will take about 30 minutes.

⋔ Moving the coals into a central spot and compacting them will create a more intense heat.

⋔ Spreading the coals out will make the heat less intense.

⋔ Red coals indicate a very hot fire.

⋔ Grey–red coals indicate a medium-heat fire.

⋔ Grey thick ash indicates a low-heat fire.

⋔ Always cook about 15 cm above the coals.

A charcoal or wood-fired barbecue with a hood with vents will create an oven-like heat. This is good for keeping food moist and will ensure more even cooking. When cooking larger pieces of food, the coals must be deep enough for the fire to last the length of the cooking time. Always follow the manufacturers' instructions on lighting and burning the coals down to get to the right heat, as well as cooking times.

Make sure you are in a safe area with no chance of starting a bushfire or harming property. Check the weather forecast for total fire bans, and remember to have water nearby in case of any emergency when cooking on open charcoal or wood barbecues.

Never leave an open fire unattended. Once you have finished cooking and are ready to pack up the barbecue site, make sure the coals or embers are put out and there is no danger of the fire starting up again – the embers should be completely cold. This is important when cooking in the bush or garden, or wherever children or pets might unknowingly burn themselves in the dying embers.

Never leave matches around where children can reach them during the cooking.

Gas-fired barbecues

Preheat gas-fired barbecues for at least 15 minutes before cooking. This will give the lava rocks and the grill or hotplate time to heat through. Once the lava rocks have heated up you can cook highly fatty foods over them with the gas flame turned off. This is also another way of keeping foods warm on the barbecue.

Setting part of the barbecue on high, part on medium and part on low will create a searing area, a medium and slow cooking area, and a finishing area. This is useful when cooking larger pieces of food that need to be seared and sealed first, and then cooked for longer over a low heat.

A gas barbecue with a lid will protect the food from wind and also means the food can be roasted, as the heat is reflected back onto the food from the cover. As in an oven, whole meals can be cooked using this method. Some barbecues have a temperature gauge on the lid that will help with judging cooking times. To be sure, use a roasting meat thermometer that can probe the food and indicate when it is ready.

Kettle barbecues

These can be either gas or charcoal and are great for roasting, particularly larger pieces of food. They can also be used for smoking food, but it pays to experiment with the smoking chips to get the flavour you like, and the best chip for different foods.

Cleaning

After cooking, and while the barbecue grill or plate is still warm, brush over a little salt or sand. This will help to absorb any grease or smells.

To clean the grill rack or plate, use a stiff wire brush to remove any hard-to-remove, cooked-on food.

When the barbecue is cold, clean it with hot soapy water, then rinse it off and dry it with newspaper. Rub some light olive oil over the grill rack and plate. This will help prevent rust forming.

Brush out the ashes from the fire, but keep any wood or charcoal beads that haven't burned and store them in a dry area until next time. Put any ashes into a compost or on the garden. Cover the barbecue with a waterproof cover or store in a dry area in the garage, shed or house.

Essential equipment for the barbecue

You will need:

⊼ Sturdy, long-handled tongs
⊼ A long-handled spatula (a new, long-handled paint scraper is a good substitute) – for turning food and scraping food debris from the barbecue plate
⊼ Long, flat metal skewers – for keeping meats butterflied flat and making them easier to turn
⊼ A hinged grill rack (keep well oiled so food doesn't stick) – mainly used for whole fish but can be used for fish fillets, sausages, chicken wings, butterflied meats and poultry
⊼ Bamboo skewers (soak in cold water before using)
⊼ A stiff wire brush – for cleaning the grill
⊼ Long-handled basting brushes made of natural fibres (nylon will melt) – rosemary branches or leafy tops of celery work well for this task
⊼ Barbecue matches

⊼ Spray water bottle – to keep any flare-up in check

⊼ Heavy-duty aluminium foil – to cover food during the last half of cooking, and for wrapping certain foods which are cooked directly on the barbecue

Beef, Lamb and Pork

Peppered Beef Fillet with Mushroom Pesto

Serves 4–6

800 g beef fillet, thick butt end
¼ cup freshly ground black pepper
a little olive oil

Mushroom Pesto
1½ cups dried shitake mushrooms
2 tablespoons soy sauce
2 cups boiling water
3 tablespoons coarsely chopped flat-leaf parsley
2 cloves garlic, finely chopped
2 green onions, finely chopped
1 tablespoon olive oil
salt and freshly ground black pepper

ᛦ Rub the beef fillet with the pepper and a little olive oil. Chill until ready to cook.

ᛦ For the Mushroom Pesto, place the mushrooms in a mixing bowl and pour over the soy sauce and boiling water. Leave for 30 minutes, until softened. Remove and drain, reserving 2 tablespoons of the soaking liquid. Place the mushrooms, parsley, garlic, onion and soaking liquid in a food processor and blend until finely chopped. With the motor still running, pour in the olive oil. Remove the pesto to a serving dish, and season with salt and freshly ground black pepper to taste.

及 Bring the beef to room temperature, preheat the barbecue to medium-high and lightly oil the grill. Cook the beef for 4–5 minutes each side, turning twice, until cooked on the outside but still pink in the middle. Remove, cover loosely with foil and allow to rest for 15 minutes. Serve with creamy mashed potatoes and the mushroom pesto.

Beef Sirloin with Mustard Caper Sauce

Serves 4

3 tablespoons olive oil
2 tablespoons dried marjoram *or* oregano leaves
1.5 kg beef sirloin, trimmed of fat

Mustard Caper Sauce
3 tablespoons Dijon mustard
3 egg yolks
1 small green onion, finely chopped
juice of ½ a lemon
1 cup light olive oil
1½ tablespoons capers, rinsed and drained
½ cup caperberries (pickled berries from the caper bush)

⊼ Mix together the olive oil and marjoram leaves and rub all over the beef. Set aside for 15 minutes.

⊼ For the mustard caper sauce, blend the mustard, egg yolks, green onion and lemon juice in a food processor until creamy. With the motor still running, slowly drizzle in the light olive oil until the mixture is thick. Remove to a bowl and stir in the capers and caperberries.

⊼ Preheat the barbecue to medium-high and lightly oil the grill. Cook the beef for 6–7 minutes each side, turning a couple of times. Remove, cover loosely with foil and allow to rest for 10 minutes before slicing. Serve with potatoes baked in foil.

Grilled Rump Steak Burritos

Serves 4

>   500 g rump steak, cut into 2 pieces and trimmed of fat
>   2 tablespoons lime juice
>   4 large floured tortillas *or* 8 small floured tortillas
>   2 small ripe avocados, peeled and mashed with a little
>   lemon juice
>   ¼ cup sour cream
>   ½ cup grated cheddar cheese
>   1 cup finely diced tomatoes

ⵔ Preheat the oven to 180°C. Place the steaks in a shallow baking dish. Pour over the lime juice and set aside for 30 minutes.

ⵔ Wrap the tortillas in foil and warm in the oven for 10 minutes.

ⵔ Meanwhile, preheat the barbecue to high and lightly oil the grill. Cook the steaks for 4–5 minutes each side. Remove and slice thinly on the diagonal.

ⵔ Remove the tortillas from the oven and onto each one place some steak slices, mashed avocado, sour cream, grated cheese and diced tomato. Roll up and serve immediately with a mixed-leaf salad on the side.

Korean-style Beef Spare Ribs

Serves 4

1.5 kg beef spare ribs

Marinade
¼ cup finely chopped green onion
3 cloves garlic, finely chopped
1 tablespoon finely grated ginger
¾ cup soy sauce
½ cup white sugar
2 tablespoons sesame oil

⽊ Cut the ribs into individual pieces, then trim and discard the excess fat. Place the ribs in a shallow baking dish. Mix together the marinade ingredients and pour over the ribs. Chill for 3 hours, turning the ribs a couple of times.

⽊ Preheat the barbecue to medium and lightly oil the grill. Remove the ribs from the marinade and pat dry. Cook the ribs for 5 minutes each side. Serve with Asian Coleslaw (page 96).

Orange and Rum-scented Baby Lamb Cutlets

Serves 4

12 baby lamb cutlets
½ cup chicken stock

Marinade
100 ml freshly squeezed orange juice
1 tablespoon honey
50 ml dark rum
¼ teaspoon grated orange zest
½ teaspoon dried rosemary leaves

𝓡 Mix together all the marinade ingredients in a shallow bowl. Add the lamb cutlets and set aside for 20 minutes.

𝓡 Preheat the barbecue to high and lightly oil the grill. Remove the lamb cutlets from the marinade and cook for 3–4 minutes each side.

𝓡 Meanwhile, add the chicken stock to the marinade and pour the mixture into a saucepan. Bring to the boil and simmer over gentle heat for 5 minutes. To serve, spoon the sauce over the lamb cutlets. Serve with Potato Pancakes (page 100) or creamy mashed potato.

Oriental Butterflied
Leg of Lamb

Serves 6–8

1 × 1.2 kg boned leg of lamb, butterflied

Marinade
1 clove garlic, finely sliced
1 teaspoon finely grated ginger
2 teaspoons ground coriander
1 teaspoon ground turmeric
3 tablespoons soy sauce
3 tablespoons rice wine vinegar
3 tablespoons olive oil
freshly ground black pepper

⊼ Trim the leg of lamb of any fat and score the meat at the thickest part with a sharp knife.

⊼ Mix together all the marinade ingredients in a small bowl, then pour into a shallow baking tin. Add the lamb and rub the marinade into the meat. Set aside for 1 hour, turning the lamb to infuse both sides.

⊼ Preheat the barbecue to medium and lightly oil the grill. Remove the lamb from the marinade and insert two metal skewers through the meat to hold it flat. Cook, skin-side up, for 15 minutes. Turn and cook for a further 10 minutes, or until the meat is still a little pink on the inside. Remove, cover loosely with foil and allow to rest for 15 minutes before carving. Serve with chargrilled vegetables and Tahini-style Sauce (page 127).

Lamb Loin Fillets with Herbs and Garlic

Serves 4

500 g lamb loin fillets
freshly ground black pepper

Herb Marinade
¾ cup red wine
½ cup soy sauce
4 cloves garlic, crushed
½ cup finely chopped mint leaves
2 tablespoons fresh rosemary leaves

⋔ Place the lamb in a shallow baking dish. Mix together the marinade ingredients and pour over the lamb. Set aside for 1 hour.

⋔ Preheat the barbecue to high and lightly oil the grill. Remove the lamb fillets from the marinade and cook for 4–5 minutes each side, until the lamb is still pink in the middle. Remove, cover loosely with foil and leave to rest for 10 minutes. Slice thinly and serve with Couscous Tabouli-style Salad (page 92).

Pork Ribs with Maple Syrup Glaze

Serves 4

1.5 kg pork ribs

Maple Syrup Glaze
1 clove garlic, finely chopped
½ teaspoon dried thyme leaves
1 teaspoon ground paprika
½ teaspoon freshly ground black pepper
½ cup maple syrup
4 tablespoons light olive oil

ᚱ Place the pork ribs in a shallow baking dish. Mix together the maple syrup glaze ingredients and pour over the ribs, making sure the ribs are covered on both sides. Chill for 2 hours.

ᚱ Preheat the barbecue to medium and lightly oil the grill. Drain the ribs from the marinade. Cook the ribs for 10–15 minutes, turning at least four times and brushing with a little of the leftover marinade. Serve immediately.

Pork Spare Ribs with Southern Texas Sauce

Serves 4

1.6 kg pork spare ribs, trimmed of fat

Southern Texas Sauce
2 tablespoons light olive oil
1 onion, finely chopped
1 large clove garlic, finely chopped
½ cup tomato sauce
½ cup cider vinegar
¼ cup Worcestershire sauce
2 teaspoons Dijon mustard
1 teaspoon salt
juice of 1 lemon

⊼ To make the sauce, heat the olive oil in a saucepan over medium heat and cook the onion and garlic for 4–5 minutes, until soft. Stir in the rest of the sauce ingredients and bring to the boil. Simmer for 15 minutes, stirring occasionally. Remove from the heat and scoop about ¼ cup of the sauce out of the pan to brush over the ribs. Reserve the rest to serve as a dipping sauce. Brush some of the ¼ cup of sauce over the pork ribs on both sides.

⊼ Preheat the barbecue to medium and lightly oil the grill. Cook the ribs for 6–8 minutes each side, turning a couple of times and brushing with a little more of the sauce as you go. Serve immediately.

Grilled Pork Leg Schnitzels with Pawpaw and Chilli Salsa

Serves 4

4 pork leg schnitzels (pork loin chops or pork fillets)
salt and freshly ground black pepper
light olive oil, for brushing

Pawpaw and Chilli Salsa
½ cup finely chopped pawpaw
½ cup finely chopped firm mango flesh
¼ cup finely chopped red pepper
1 small red onion, finely chopped
1 small red chilli, finely chopped
2 tablespoons finely chopped fresh coriander leaves
1 tablespoon lime or lemon juice

🍖 To make the pawpaw and chilli salsa, combine all the salsa ingredients in a bowl and mix well. Chill until ready to serve.

🍖 Preheat the barbecue to medium and lightly oil the grill. Season the pork with salt and pepper to taste, and brush with a little light olive oil. Cook the schnitzels for 3–4 minutes each side, depending on the thickness. Serve with the salsa spooned over the top, and potatoes baked in foil on the side.

Poultry and Fowl

Whole Chicken Butterflied with Pancetta and Olive Butter

Serves 4

1 × 1.5 kg chicken
light olive oil, for cooking

Stuffing
¼ cup finely chopped pancetta
1 clove garlic, finely chopped
6 kalamata olives, stoned and roughly chopped
1 tablespoon finely chopped fresh parsley
100 g unsalted butter, softened

卉 Cut the chicken down the backbone with kitchen scissors and open it out. Trim away the backbone and discard (or reserve to make chicken stock).

卉 Mash the stuffing ingredients together in a bowl until well combined.

卉 With your fingers, carefully lift the skin from the neck end of the chicken, making a pocket across the breasts and down to the leg and thigh on each side. Insert the stuffing into this area underneath the skin and carefully push the skin down to flatten out the stuffing. Chill while you prepare the barbecue.

Preheat the barbecue to medium–high and lightly oil the grill. Brush the chicken with a little oil. Cook, skin-side down, for 5–6 minutes. Turn the chicken over and cook for a further 30 minutes, basting the chicken from time to time with a little oil, until the juices run clear when the thickest part is pierced with a skewer. Remove, cover loosely with foil and allow to rest for 10 minutes. Serve with White Bean Purée (page 102) and a green salad.

Chicken Maryland with Chilli Herb Spice Rub

Serves 4

1 teaspoon ground chilli
2 teaspoons ground paprika
1 teaspoon dried thyme leaves
1 teaspoon ground marjoram
4 chicken Maryland pieces *or* **chicken thighs**

⋔ Mix the spices and herbs together and rub all over the chicken.

⋔ Preheat the barbecue to medium and lightly oil the grill. Cook the chicken, skin-side down, for 15 minutes. Turn over and cook for a further 20 minutes, until the juices run clear when the thickest part is pierced with a skewer. Remove and serve with Sweet Red Onions with Raisins and Balsamic Vinegar (page 85) and barbecued baby corn.

Grilled Chicken with Cheese and Herb Stuffing

Serves 4

4 large single chicken breasts, skin on
2 teaspoons lemon pepper seasoning
olive oil, for brushing
200 g orzo (small rice-shaped pasta)
2 tablespoons finely grated parmesan

Stuffing
125 g soft goat's cheese *or* **feta**
1 tablespoon finely chopped fresh parsley
1 egg yolk
½ cup chopped stoned kalamata olives

柷 With a fork, mix together the stuffing ingredients in a bowl.

柷 Using two fingers, gently ease the skin off the flesh of the chicken breasts to make a pocket, starting at the short end of the fillet. Carefully push about 1 tablespoon of stuffing into the pocket and gently press down on the skin to flatten out the stuffing. Chill the chicken for 30 minutes.

柷 Preheat the barbecue to medium–high and lightly oil the grill. Rub the lemon pepper seasoning over the chicken and brush with olive oil. Cook, skin-side down, for 6–7 minutes. Turn over and cook for a further 4 minutes, or until the chicken is cooked through. Serve immediately with orzo and parmesan.

Rolled Chicken Breasts with Prunes and Water Chestnuts

Serves 4

2 double chicken breasts, skin on and bone removed
3–4 tablespoons dry white wine *or* chicken stock
a little olive oil
freshly ground black pepper

Stuffing
8 pitted prunes, roughly chopped
8 water chestnuts, roughly chopped
½ teaspoon finely grated lemon zest
1 green onion, finely chopped
½ cup fresh breadcrumbs
pinch of freshly grated nutmeg

Remove the tenderloins from the chicken breast fillets and reserve for kebabs or to make chicken stock.

Lie the chicken breasts between two pieces of baking paper and gently pound with a meat mallet to flatten them out a little.

Mix together the stuffing ingredients in a bowl, then moisten with wine or chicken stock.

Spread the stuffing evenly onto the two double chicken breasts. Carefully roll each one up and secure with kitchen string to make a neat roll. Chill while you prepare the barbecue.

⼋ Preheat the barbecue to medium-high and lightly oil the grill. Brush a little oil on the outside of the chicken rolls and season with freshly ground black pepper to taste. Cook for 4–5 minutes each side, turning to brown on all sides, until the juices run clear when the thickest part is pierced with a skewer. Remove, cover loosely with foil and allow to rest for 10 minutes. Serve with Lemon Pepper Pilaf (page 98) and a green salad.

Festive Barbecued Turkey Breast with Spinach, Feta and Red Peppers

Serves 8–10

>   3 medium-sized red peppers, cut in half, seeds and
>   membranes removed
>   500 g English spinach
>   200 g feta
>   ½ teaspoon dried rosemary
>   ½ teaspoon dried thyme
>   freshly ground black pepper
>   1 boned turkey breast (about 1.65 kg)
>   6 slices pancetta
>   a little light olive oil

ⴷ   Preheat the barbecue to high and chargrill the peppers, skin-side down, until blistered and blackened. Remove from the heat and place in a plastic bag to cool. When cool enough to handle, peel the skins off and cut into strips.

ⴷ   Wash the spinach and remove the stalks. Do not spin the water off. Reserving six leaves, cook the spinach in a covered saucepan over medium heat for 1–2 minutes, until wilted. Remove and squeeze out most of the moisture by placing the spinach in a sieve and pushing down with a large spoon. Chop the spinach and mix in a bowl with the feta and herbs. Season with freshly ground black pepper to taste.

ⴷ   Using a sharp knife, cut the turkey breast lengthways to open it out. Lie the reserved spinach leaves down the centre, then lay the capsicum strips over the leaves. Spread over the spinach mixture and use your hands or a spoon to form a log of mixture down the middle. Carefully bring the sides together. Wrap the pancetta slices around the turkey breast and tie securely with string. Rub the meat with a little oil.

⩗ Preheat the barbecue to medium–low and lightly oil the grill. Cook the turkey breast, skin-side down, with the top side covered in foil, for 30 minutes. Remove the foil, turn the breast over and cover the new top side with foil. Cook for a further 20 minutes, until the juices run clear when the thickest part is pierced with a skewer. Remove, cover loosely with foil and allow to rest for 20 minutes before carving. Remove the string and slice the meat. This is delicious served cold or hot.

Grilled Turkey Fillet Sandwiches

Serves 4

> **4 turkey breast schnitzels** *or* **small chicken breast fillets,**
> **pounded flat**
> **light olive oil, for cooking**
> **salt and freshly ground black pepper**
> **50 g melted butter**
> **8 slices rye bread**
> **2 cups finely shredded green cabbage**
> **½ cup Aïoli (page 118)**
> **8 thin slices Swiss cheese**

器 Preheat the barbecue to high and lightly oil the grill. Cook the turkey schnitzels or chicken fillets for 3–4 minutes each side, brushing with a little oil during the cooking. Season with salt and freshly ground black pepper to taste.

器 Brush the melted butter on one side of each slice of rye bread. Mix the shredded cabbage into the Aïoli. Top the unbuttered side of four slices of bread with the Swiss cheese, then add the cooked turkey schnitzels and the cabbage mayonnaise. Cover with the unbuttered sides of the remaining slices of bread. Stick a wooden toothpick through the middle of each sandwich to help hold them together.

器 Cook the assembed sandwiches on the preheated barbecue for 2–3 minutes each side, until the cheese starts to melt. Serve immediately.

Herb-scented Butterflied Poussin

Serves 4-6

4 × 350–400 g poussin
½ cup mixed fresh herbs (such as thyme, rosemary, parsley
** and marjoram), roughly chopped**
2 cloves garlic, smashed and cut into small slivers
1–2 tablespoons olive oil

⋔ To prepare the poussin, cut through the back of the carcass and open out. Remove the back rib cage, wing tips, neck and gizzards (these can be frozen to make stock). With a sharp knife, slash the legs at the thickest part, as well as the breast area.

⋔ Mix the herbs, garlic and oil together in a bowl. Rub into the poussin on both sides and set aside for 30 minutes.

⋔ Preheat the barbecue to medium–high and lightly oil the grill. Cook the poussin directly on the grill, breast-side down, for 6 minutes. Turn over and cook for a further 3–4 minutes. To test whether the birds are cooked, pierce the thickest part of the leg with a skewer – the juices should run clear. Remove to a platter and serve with lemon wedges, grilled eggplant and Potato Pancakes (page 100).

Asian Spiced Barbecued Quail

Serves 4–6

8 quail, butterflied

Marinade
100 ml freshly squeezed lime juice
¼ cup brown sugar
¼ cup olive oil
1 teaspoon chilli paste
3 cloves garlic, finely chopped
¼ cup finely chopped green onion

⬸ Place the butterflied quail in a baking dish. Mix together the marinade ingredients and pour over the quail. Chill for 1 hour, turning once.

⬸ Preheat the barbecue to medium and lightly oil the grill. Cook the quail, meat-side down, for 6 minutes. Turn over, baste with the marinade and cook for a further 6–8 minutes, or until the juices run clear when the thickest part is pierced with a skewer. Remove and cut in half again with poultry shears or a sharp knife. Serve on a bed of baby rocket and decorate with lime wedges.

Chinese Spiced Duck Breasts

Serves 4

> **4 × 125–150 g duck breasts**
> **½ teaspoon Chinese five-spice powder**
> **½ teaspoon ground ginger**
> **¼ teaspoon ground chilli**
> **1 tablespoon plum sauce**
> **2 tablespoons lime juice**

Score the skin of the duck breasts with a knife, cutting diagonally to make a diamond pattern and taking care not to pierce the breast flesh. Mix the spices together and rub all over the duck breasts. Cover and chill until ready to cook.

Mix together the plum sauce and lime juice in a bowl.

Preheat the barbecue to medium and brush the skin of the duck breasts with some of the plum sauce mixture. Cook, skin-side down, for 5–6 minutes, until the skin is crispy. Turn over, brush with more of the plum sauce mixture and cook for a further 8 minutes for rare duck, or 10 minutes for medium/well-done. Remove, slice and serve with Hokkien Noodles with Mushrooms and Chinese Cabbage (page 97).

Seafood

Whole Fish with Lime Ginger Marinade

Serves 4

> **2 whole fish, about 500 g each (snapper, red mullet,
>   silver perch, barramundi), cleaned and gutted**
> **salt and freshly ground black pepper**
>
> Marinade
> **zest of 1 lime, freshly grated**
> **6 tablespoons freshly squeezed lime juice (about 3 limes)**
> **1 large clove garlic, finely chopped**
> **1 tablespoon freshly grated ginger**
> **¼ cup olive oil**

꼬 Slash the fish with a sharp knife at the thickest part, near the head, on both sides of the fish. Rub these cavities with a little salt and pepper. Mix together the marinade ingredients and pour half over the fish. Marinate for 1 hour in the fridge until ready to cook. Reserve the rest of the marinade for basting and serving.

꼬 Preheat the barbecue to high and lightly oil the plate. Make two straps of triple thickness from heavy-duty foil to go around each fish. Twist the end of each strap to form handles to lift and turn the fish over with during the cooking.

꼬 Cook the fish for 4–5 minutes each side, basting a little with the reserved marinade. To test whether it is cooked, pierce the thickest part of the fish with a knife – the flesh should move easily. Remove and take the foil straps off. Serve immediately with a little marinade spooned over, and with lime wedges and Aïoli (page 118) on the side.

Tandoori Spiced Whole Fish

Serves 4

4 whole fish, about 300 g each (red mullet, small bream, silver perch, leather jacket), cleaned and gutted

Tandoori Spice Mix
1 teaspoon ground coriander
1 teaspoon ground cumin
1 tablespoon ground paprika
1 teaspoon ground cinnamon
1 teaspoon ground ginger
1 teaspoon ground turmeric
1 teaspoon ground chilli
1 tablespoon white vinegar
1 tablespoon plain yoghurt

ㅠ Combine the Tandoori spice mix ingredients in a bowl. Make a few slashes in the thickest part of each fish, on both sides, and brush the spice mix over the fish. Marinate for 1 hour in the fridge.

ㅠ Preheat the barbecue to medium and lightly oil the grill. Cook the fish for 4–5 minutes each side, until cooked through. Remove and serve with Asian Coleslaw (page 96).

Barbecued Whole Fish with Fennel Spice Rub

Serves 4

2 whole barramundi, snapper or silver perch *or* other firm
medium-sized fish (500 g each), cleaned and gutted
salt and freshly ground black pepper

Spice Rub
1 tablespoon dry-roasted fennel seeds
1 tablespoon dry-roasted coriander seeds
1 teaspoon ground tumeric
1 teaspoon cayenne pepper
1 tablespoon sea salt

ℛ Slash each fish with a sharp knife at the thickest part, near the head, on both sides of the fish. Rub these cavities with a little salt and pepper.

ℛ Mix the spice rub together in a mortar and pestle and grind to a rough paste. Rub all over the fish, inside and outside.

ℛ Preheat the barbecue to high and lightly oil the plate. Make two straps of triple thickness from heavy-duty foil to go around each fish. Twist the end of each strap to form handles to lift and turn the fish over with during the cooking. Alternatively, put the fish into a well-oiled hinged barbecue basket.

ℛ Cook the fish for 4–5 minutes each side, brushing with a little oil. To test whether it is cooked, pierce the thickest part with a knife – the flesh should move easily. Remove and take the foil straps off. Serve immediately.

—< Tip: To dry-roast whole spices, heat a saucepan over high heat for 2 minutes, place the spices into the pan and stir for 1 minute. Remove from the heat and shake until the spices start to smoke. Remove the spices from the pan to a mortar and pestle. Dry roasting develops the oils and gives a delicious smoky flavour.

Whole Sardines Grilled with Caperberry Salsa

Serves 4

16 whole sardines, cleaned and gutted
a little olive oil
salt and pepper

Caperberry Salsa
¼ cup caperberries (pickled berries from the caper bush),
   drained and roughly chopped
2 teaspoons grated lemon zest
4 tablespoons chopped green onions
¼ cup kalamata olives, stoned and roughly chopped
2 tablespoons virgin olive oil
1 tablespoon red wine vinegar

뮤 Mix the caperberry salsa ingredients in a bowl and set aside until ready to serve.

뮤 Preheat the barbecue to high and oil the plate. Brush each sardine with oil and season with salt and pepper. Cook for 2–3 minutes each side, until lightly browned. Serve immediately with the caperberry salsa and a mixed-leaf salad.

Grilled Fish in Banana Leaves

Serves 4

500 g redfish, ling *or* gemfish, cut into chunks
1 tablespoon finely chopped fresh ginger
1 large green chilli, deseeded and finely chopped
1 tablespoon finely chopped coriander stalks
2 tablespoons finely chopped coriander leaves
1 teaspoon salt
½ teaspoon ground turmeric
1 teaspoon chilli paste
1 tablespoon cornflour
1 egg, lightly beaten
2 tablespoons coconut cream
1 banana leaf, cut into 8 pieces (about 12 × 15 cm
rectangles)

闲 In a food processor, blend all the ingredients except the banana leaf
to make a smooth paste. Make small parcels by wrapping about ¼ cup
of the fish paste in each banana leaf piece. Secure each parcel with a
toothpick. Chill until ready to cook.

闲 Preheat the barbecue to medium–high and lightly oil the grill.
Cook the fish parcels for 4–5 minutes each side, until cooked through.
Remove and serve with Lemon Pepper Pilaf (page 98).

Barbecued Peppered Tuna

Serves 4

2 tablespoons light olive oil
600 g tuna fillet (*or* swordfish *or* salmon fillets), cut into
   4 thick steaks
1 tablespoon salt
5 tablespoons freshly cracked black pepper

穴 Brush the oil over the fish steaks. Mix the salt and pepper together and rub all over the steaks.

穴 Preheat the barbecue to medium and lightly oil the grill. Cook the steaks for 2–3 minutes each side for rare, or 4–5 minutes for medium. Remove and serve with Roasted Tomato Relish (page 120) and White Bean Purée (page 102).

TIP: Tuna is best cooked medium, as it can dry out if overcooked. Cooking times will depend on the thickness of the fish.

Grilled Marinated Sea Perch Fillets in Vine Leaves

Serves 4

4 sea perch fillets, about 180 g each
salt and pepper
8 vine leaves (fresh, or if in brine, well rinsed)
olive oil spray

Marinade
1 tablespoon virgin olive oil
1 clove garlic, finely chopped
1 teaspoon grated orange zest
1 tablespoon finely chopped stuffed olives

Cut the fish fillets in half and place in a shallow bowl. Mix together the marinade ingredients and spread most of it over the fillets. Marinate for about 30 minutes in the fridge, until ready to cook. Wash or drain the vine leaves and set aside.

Preheat the barbecue to high and lightly oil the grill. Wrap each fillet with the remaining marinade in a vine leaf, and secure with a toothpick. Spray a little olive oil over the leaves and cook for 2–3 minutes each side, until firm to touch. Serve immediately with Greek-style Salad (page 93) and crusty bread.

Grilled Swordfish Fillets wrapped in Prosciutto with Baby Spinach Pesto

Serves 4

4 swordfish fillets, about 150 g each, cut about 3 cm thick
4 slices prosciutto
olive oil, for brushing

Baby Spinach Pesto
3 tablespoons olive oil
2 cups baby spinach (about 200 g)
4 cloves garlic
2 tablespoons finely grated parmesan
2 tablespoons pine nuts

ߘ Wrap each swordfish fillet with a piece of prosciutto and secure with a toothpick.

ߘ For the spinach pesto, heat the oil in a frying pan and wilt the spinach leaves. Remove to a food processor and blend with the garlic, parmesan and pine nuts. Set aside until ready to serve.

ߘ Preheat the barbecue to hot and lightly brush the fillets with oil. Cook for 3–4 minutes each side and serve immediately with the pesto spooned over the top of the fish.

Grilled Marinated Octopus

Serves 4

16 baby octopus

Marinade
2 cloves garlic, finely chopped
½ cup olive oil
juice of ½ lemon
1 tablespoon finely chopped flat-leaf parsley
1 green onion, finely chopped
2 tablespoons red wine

⋔ Clean the octopus and remove beak and guts. Mix the marinade ingredients together in a bowl and add the octopus. Cover and let stand for 2 hours.

⋔ Preheat the barbecue to hot and lightly oil the grill. Drain the octopus from the marinade and cook for 4–6 minutes, until pink and lightly browned. Serve immediately with tossed mixed-leaf salad, lemon wedges and crusty bread.

Japanese-style Stuffed Squid Hoods with Vegetables

Serves 4

4 medium-sized squid hoods
1 small carrot, peeled and cut into small pieces
8 baby French beans, topped and tailed and cut into
small pieces
4 green onions, trimmed and finely chopped
2 eggs, lightly beaten
½ teaspoon sesame oil

Ӿ Clean the squid hoods under running cold water and set aside.

Ӿ Blanch the carrot and beans for 2 minutes, then refresh under cold water and drain. Mix with the green onion, egg and sesame oil. Heat a non-stick frying pan over medium heat and pour in the egg and vegetable mixture. Cook for 2–3 minutes, until nearly set. Remove to a bowl and cool.

Ӿ Spoon the egg and vegetable mixture into the squid hoods and secure the end of each hood with a toothpick. Refrigerate until ready to cook.

Ӿ Preheat the barbecue to medium–high and lightly oil the plate. Cook the squid for 3–4 minutes each side. Serve immediately with rice and Soy Ginger Dipping Sauce (page 127).

Grilled Bugs with Mustard Butter

Serves 4

8 medium-sized uncooked bugs (Balmain or Moreton Bay)
Mustard Butter (page 128)
a little butter

Cut the bugs in half lengthways and remove any stomach vein and guts.

Preheat the barbecue to high and lightly oil the grill. Cook the bugs, shell-side up, for 2–3 minutes. Turn the bugs over and brush a little of the mustard butter over the flesh. Cook for a further 2–3 minutes, until the flesh is cooked through. Remove and melt a little butter over the bug flesh. Serve immediately with a mixed-leaf salad and Spicy Potato Wedges (page 83).

Burgers

Tasty Beef Burgers

Serves 4–6

1 teaspoon salt
½ teaspoon freshly ground black pepper
600 g coarsely minced beef
4–6 hamburger buns
olive oil, for brushing

⟆ Mix together the salt, pepper and minced meat and shape into four to six plump burgers. Chill for 30 minutes while you prepare the barbecue.

⟆ Preheat the barbecue to medium–high and lightly oil the grill. Cook the burgers for 4–5 minutes each side for rare, 6–7 for medium or 7–8 minutes for well done.

⟆ While the burgers are cooking, slice the hamburger buns in half and brush lightly with oil. Grill, cut-side down, until lightly browned. Remove and fill with green salad and the cooked burgers. Serve immediately with Aïoli (page 118) or tomato sauce, or coarse-grain mustard.

Variations

Peppercrust Burgers
Sprinkle the shaped burgers each side with ¼ teaspoon coarsely ground black pepper before cooking.

Cheesy Surprise Burgers
Insert into the centre of each of the shaped burgers 1 small cube feta, blue cheese, brie *or* 1 tablespoon grated mozzarella before cooking.

Herbed Beef Burgers
Add to the burger mixture 1 tablespoon finely chopped fresh chives,
1 tablespoon finely chopped fresh parsley, 1 tablespoon finely chopped
fresh basil and 1 finely chopped clove garlic before cooking.

Teriyaki Beef Burgers
Add to the burger mixture 2 tablespoons dry sherry, 2 tablespoons
soy sauce, 1 finely chopped clove garlic, 1 teaspoon finely grated ginger
and 1 tablespoon finely chopped green onion before cooking.

Lamb Burgers with Pocket Bread

Serves 4

**600 g minced lamb (from neck or shoulder, with
 15 per cent fat)**
1 tablespoon finely chopped fresh parsley
1 teaspoon finely chopped fresh oregano
1 clove garlic, finely chopped
1 teaspoon salt
freshly ground black pepper
4 small pocket breads

☐ Mix all the ingredients except the pocket breads together and shape into four to six round burgers. Chill for 30 minutes while you prepare the barbecue.

☐ Preheat the barbecue to medium–high and lightly oil the grill. Cook the burgers for 6–7 minutes each side for medium, or 8–9 minutes for well done.

☐ Split the pocket breads in half, add some green salad and sit the cooked burgers inside. Serve with Mint and Coriander Mayonnaise (page 121).

Variations

Surprise Burgers
Insert into each of the shaped burgers ¼ cup roughly chopped black olives, ¼ cup roughly chopped fresh parsley, ½ cup cooked diced bacon, ¼ cup mustard, ¼ cup fruit pickle, ¼ cup roughly chopped semi-dried tomatoes *or* 4 large pitted prunes, and 4 sage leaves before cooking.

Morrocan-style Burgers

Add to the burger mixture 1 teaspoon allspice, ½ teaspoon ground cinnamon, ½ teaspoon ground chilli and ¼ cup finely chopped green onion before cooking.

Spicy Lamb Burgers

Serves 4

> 1 kg lean minced lamb
> 1 large carrot, peeled and finely grated
> 1 large zucchini, finely grated
> 1 teaspoon finely minced ginger
> 1 teaspoon finely grated lemon zest
> 1 small onion, finely chopped
> 1 teaspoon chilli paste
> 1 tablespoon finely chopped fresh parsley
> 4 tablespoons fresh breadcrumbs
> 1 egg
> salt and freshly ground black pepper, to taste
> 4 hamburger buns
> olive oil, for brushing

ᗒ Mix all the ingredients except the buns and oil together, and shape into four to six round burgers. Chill for 30 minutes while you prepare the barbecue.

ᗒ Preheat the barbecue to medium–high and lightly oil the grill. Cook the burgers for 6–7 minutes each side for medium, or 8–9 minutes for well done.

ᗒ While the burgers are cooking, slice the hamburger buns in half and brush lightly with oil. Grill, cut-side down, until lightly browned. Remove and fill with green salad and the cooked burgers. Serve with a Spicy Tomato Relish (page 120).

Pork and Veal Burgers with Apple Relish

Serves 4

600 g minced pork and veal
¼ cup finely chopped green onion
1 teaspoon Italian dried herbs
½ teaspoon grated lemon zest
1 tablespoon olive oil
4 hamburger buns
olive oil, extra, for brushing
apple relish, to serve

஡ Mix all the ingredients except the buns and extra oil together in a bowl. Chill for 1 hour. Shape the mixture into four burgers and return to the fridge while you prepare the barbecue.

஡ Preheat the barbecue to medium and lightly oil the grill. Cook the burgers for 8–10 minutes each side, until cooked through.

஡ While the burgers are cooking, slice the hamburger buns in half and brush lightly with oil. Grill, cut-side down, until lightly browned. Remove and fill with green salad and the cooked burgers. Serve with apple relish.

Chicken Burgers with Fruit Chutney

Serves 4

600 g chicken thigh fillet
   ***or* bought minced chicken (with 15 per cent fat)**
1 tablespoon finely chopped green onion
1 tablespoon fresh lemon thyme leaves
2 cloves garlic, finely minced
1 tablespoon finely chopped flat-leaf parsley
1 tablespoon olive oil
1 teaspoon white pepper
pinch of salt
4 hamburger buns
olive oil, extra, for brushing
fruit chutney, to serve

⚎ If using whole chicken fillets, mince them first in a food processor until coarsely chopped. Remove to a bowl and mix in the rest of the ingredients except the buns and extra oil. Chill for at least 1 hour. Shape the mixture into four burgers and return to the fridge while you prepare the barbecue.

⚎ Preheat the barbecue to medium–high and lightly oil the grill. Cook the burgers for 6–8 minutes each side, until done.

⚎ While the burgers are cooking, slice the hamburger buns in half and brush lightly with oil. Grill, cut-side down, until lightly browned. Remove and fill with green salad and the cooked burgers. Serve with fruit chutney.

Turkey Burgers with Cranberry Relish

Serves 4

600 g turkey breast or thigh fillet
1 medium-sized onion, grated
1 teaspoon Tabasco sauce
1 tablespoon finely chopped flat-leaf parsley
1 tablespoon olive oil
1 teaspoon white pepper
½ teaspoon salt
pinch of salt
4 hamburger buns
olive oil, extra, for brushing
cranberry relish, to serve

⚟ Coarsely mince the turkey meat in a food processor. Remove to a bowl and mix in the rest of the ingredients except the buns and extra oil. Chill for 1 hour. Shape the mixture into four burgers and return to the fridge while you prepare the barbecue.

⚟ Preheat the barbecue to medium and lightly oil the grill. Cook the burgers for 8–10 minutes each side, until cooked through.

⚟ While the burgers are cooking, slice the hamburger buns in half and brush lightly with oil. Grill, cut-side down, until lightly browned. Remove and fill with green salad and the cooked burgers. Serve with cranberry relish.

Fresh Tuna Burgers with Wasabi Mayonnaise

Serves 4

600 g fresh tuna fillet
2 teaspoons finely chopped green onion
1 teaspoon finely grated ginger
1 tablespoon finely chopped flat-leaf parsley
1 tablespoon extra-virgin olive oil
½ teaspoon salt
½ teaspoon white pepper
4 hamburger buns
olive oil, extra, for brushing

卉 Using a very sharp knife, trim any dark bloody bits from the tuna and cut away any skin. Roughly chop the fillet and place in a bowl. Mix in the green onion, ginger, parsley, extra-virgin olive oil and seasonings. Chill for 1 hour. Shape the mixture into four burgers and return to the fridge while you prepare the barbecue.

卉 Preheat the barbecue to medium–high and lightly oil the grill. Cook the burgers for 3–4 minutes each side for rare, or 4–5 minutes for medium.

卉 While the burgers are cooking, slice the hamburger buns in half and brush lightly with oil. Grill, cut-side down, until lightly browned. Spread a little Wasabi Mayonnaise (page 121) on both sides of the buns and fill with watercress leaves and the cooked burgers.

Atlantic Salmon Burgers with Dill Mustard Sauce

Serves 4

600 g Atlantic salmon fillet, bones and skin removed
1 tablespoon finely chopped green onion
2 tablespoons olive oil
1 teaspoon finely grated lemon zest
1 tablespoon finely chopped fresh dill
½ teaspoon white pepper
pinch of salt
4 hamburger buns
olive oil, extra, for brushing

 Roughly chop the salmon fillet and place in a bowl. Mix in the rest of the ingredients except the buns and extra oil. Chill for at least 1 hour. Shape the mixture into four burgers and return to the fridge while you prepare the barbecue.

 Preheat the barbecue to medium–high and lightly oil the grill. Cook the burgers for 3–4 minutes for rare, 4–5 minutes for medium or 6–8 minutes for well done.

 While the burgers are cooking, slice the hamburger buns in half and brush lightly with oil. Grill, cut-side down, until lightly browned. Remove and fill with green salad and the cooked burgers. Serve with Dill Mustard Sauce (page 124).

Indian Spiced Chickpea Burgers with Tahini-style Sauce

Serves 4

1 tablespoon light olive oil
1 onion, finely chopped
1 garlic clove, finely chopped
2 teaspoon mild Indian curry powder
1 cup chopped baby spinach (about 100 g)
1 × 440 g tin cooked chickpeas, drained
2 tablespoon finely chopped fresh coriander
2 tablespoons finely chopped fresh parsley
100 g roasted cashew nuts, finely chopped
100 g dry breadcrumbs
juice of 1 lime
2 eggs, lightly beaten
4 small pocket breads
olive oil, extra, for brushing

⅄ Heat the light olive oil in a frying pan and sauté the onion and garlic over low heat until the onion is soft. Stir in the curry powder and spinach and cook for 2–3 minutes, until the spinach has wilted.

⅄ Blend the chickpeas in a food processor until coarsely chopped. Remove to a bowl and stir in the spinach mixture, along with the rest of the ingredients except the pocket breads and extra oil. Chill for 1 hour. Shape the mixture into six small burgers and return to the fridge while you prepare the barbecue.

丼 Preheat the barbecue to medium and lightly oil the grill and the burgers. Cook the burgers for 8–10 minutes each side, until browned and heated through.

丼 While the burgers are cooking, slice the pocket breads in half and brush lightly with oil. Grill, cut-side down, until lightly browned. Remove and fill with green salad and the cooked burgers. Serve with Tahini-style Sauce (page 127).

Field Mushroom Burgers

Serves 4

2 tablespoons olive oil
1 onion, finely chopped
200 g flat field mushrooms, finely chopped
1 teaspoon fresh thyme leaves
1 tablespoon finely chopped fresh parsley
1 egg, lightly beaten
1 cup fresh breadcrumbs
1 tablespoon finely chopped toasted almonds
80 g tasty cheddar cheese, grated
2 tablespoons finely grated parmesan
salt and freshly ground black pepper
4 hamburger buns
olive oil, extra, for brushing

〣 Heat the oil in a frying pan and sauté the onion until soft, then stir in the mushrooms and herbs and cook for 3–4 minutes. Remove to a bowl and stir in the egg, breadcrumbs, almonds and cheeses, and season with salt and pepper to taste. Shape the mixture into four burgers and chill for 30 minutes while you prepare the barbecue.

〣 Preheat the barbecue to high and lightly oil the grill and the burgers. Cook the burgers for 3–4 minutes each side, until lightly browned.

〣 While the burgers are cooking, slice the hamburger buns in half and brush lightly with oil. Grill, cut-side down, until lightly browned. Remove and fill with green salad and the cooked burgers. Serve with Roasted Tomato Relish (page 120).

Mixed Bean and Chickpea Burgers

Serves 6

> 1 × 425 g tin cooked red kidney beans, rinsed and drained
> 1 × 240 g tin cooked cannellini beans, rinsed and drained
> 1 small onion, finely grated
> 1 teaspoon finely grated ginger
> 2 tablespoons Worcestershire sauce
> 1 egg, lightly beaten
> 1 × 240 g tin cooked chickpeas, rinsed and drained
> ¼ cup finely chopped fresh flat-leaf parsley
> 100 g fresh breadcrumbs
> salt and freshly ground black pepper
> 6 hamburger buns
> olive oil, for brushing

𝍐 Blend the beans together in a food processor, then add the onion, ginger, Worcestershire sauce and egg. Remove to a bowl and stir in the chickpeas, parsley and breadcrumbs. Season with salt and pepper to taste. Shape the mixture into six round burgers. Chill for 30 minutes while you prepare the barbecue.

𝍐 Preheat the barbecue to high and lightly oil the grill and the burgers. Cook the burgers for 5–6 minutes each side, until lightly browned and heated through.

𝍐 While the burgers are cooking, slice the hamburger buns in half and brush lightly with oil. Grill, cut-side down, until lightly browned. Remove and fill with rocket leaves and the cooked burgers. Serve with Spicy Tomato Relish (page 120).

Kebabs

Moroccan Ground Beef on Rosemary Skewers

Serves 4

1 kg lean, coarsely minced beef
½ teaspoon freshly grated nutmeg
½ teaspoon ground cloves
½ teaspoon ground cinnamon
½ teaspoon ground allspice
12 woody rosemary branches with tufts of leaves
   (soaked in water for 20 minutes)

祝 Mix the beef with all the spices until well combined. Lightly oil your hands and, dividing the mixture into 12, shape the mince around the rosemary branches. Chill for 30 minutes while you prepare the barbecue.

祝 Preheat the barbecue to medium–high and lightly oil the grill. Cook the skewers for 4–5 minutes each side, turning to brown and cook all sides. The meat should be a little pink inside. Remove and serve with Couscous Tabouli-style Salad (page 92) and a fruit chutney.

Skewered Beef Rolls with Green Onions

Serves 4

600 g sirloin *or* **Scotch fillet, trimmed of fat**
12 green onions, washed and stripped
8 wooden skewers (soaked in hot water for 20 minutes)

Marinade
4 tablespoons mirin *or* **dry sherry**
1 teaspoon freshly grated ginger
3 tablespoons light soy sauce
1 teaspoon sugar

⋔ Chill the meat in the freezer for 30 minutes. Remove and, with a very sharp knife, cut as thinly as possible to make about 24 slices.

⋔ Mix together the marinade ingredients and pour over the steak. Set aside for 30 minutes.

⋔ Preheat the barbecue to high and lightly oil the grill. Cut the green onions in half lengthways and wrap a slice of meat around each onion. Thread three meat and onion rolls onto each skewer. Cook the kebabs for 3–4 minutes each side. Remove and serve with Teriyaki Eggplant Slices (page 89).

Asian Beef Satay

Serves 4

500 g scotch fillet, trimmed of fat
16 wooden skewers (soaked in hot water for 20 minutes)

Marinade
1 cup coconut milk
1 teaspoon ground turmeric
1 teaspoon Thai green curry paste
2 teaspoons fish sauce

Satay Sauce
2 tablespoons Thai green curry paste
1 cup coconut cream
3 tablespoons crunchy peanut butter
1 tablespoon lime juice

尺 Cut the beef fillet into four slices, then cut each slice into four thin strips. Thread one strip onto each skewer. Mix together all the marinade ingredients and pour over the meat. Chill for 1 hour, turning once to coat all the skewers.

尺 For the sauce, place the curry paste in a small saucepan and cook for 1–2 minutes over medium heat. Pour in the coconut cream and add the peanut butter. Stir well to combine. Add the lime juice and set aside in a serving bowl.

尺 Preheat the barbecue to high and lightly oil the grill. Cook the skewers for 1–2 minutes each side, until lightly browned. Remove and serve with the warm satay sauce and boiled rice.

Persian Spiced Lamb Kebabs with Harissa

Serves 4

500 g lean, finely minced lamb
1 large onion, peeled and grated
1 egg, lightly whisked
1 teaspoon salt
freshly ground black pepper
¼ teaspoon ground allspice
¼ teaspoon ground cinnamon
12 wooden skewers (soaked in hot water for 20 minutes)

⊼ Mix together all the kebab ingredients until well combined.

⊼ Shape the mixture into 12 sausage shapes. Skewer each sausage lengthways through the middle and press to stick the meat to the sticks. Chill until ready to cook.

⊼ Preheat the barbecue to medium–high and lightly oil the grill. Cook the skewers for 3–4 minutes each side, until browned and cooked through. Serve with flat bread, salad and Harissa (page 126) on the side.

Italian-style Mixed Meat Kebabs

Serves 4

300 g pork fillet, cut into 8 cubes
3 chicken thigh fillets, cut into 8 pieces
1 lamb backstrap fillet, cut into 8 pieces
4 slices bacon, each cut into 4 pieces
8 fresh sage leaves
3–4 juniper berries, crushed
1 teaspoon crushed fennel seeds
2 tablespoons olive oil
freshly ground black pepper
8 wooden skewers (soaked in hot water for 20 minutes)

⋔ Thread a piece of pork, chicken and lamb onto each skewer, with a slice of bacon in between each piece and a fresh sage leaf somewhere near the centre of the skewer. Mix together the crushed juniper berries, fennel seeds and olive oil and brush over the kebabs. Season with pepper and chill until ready to cook.

⋔ Preheat the barbecue to high and lightly oil the grill. Cook the kebabs for 4–6 minutes each side, until browned and the meat is cooked through. Serve with Orzo with Fresh Parmesan and Basil (page 101) and Roasted Tomato Relish (page 120).

Pork, Sage and Prune Kebabs

Serves 4

> 300 g pork shoulder *or* loin, cut into cubes
> 16 prunes, pitted
> 16 fresh sage leaves
> 1 large red onion, cut into quarters
> light olive oil, for brushing
> freshly ground black pepper
> 8 wooden skewers (soaked in hot water for 20 minutes)

ㅈ Thread each skewer with a piece of pork, a pitted prune, a sage leaf and an onion quarter. Repeat, ending up with an onion quarter. Brush a little oil over the kebabs and season well with pepper.

ㅈ Preheat the barbecue to medium–high and lightly oil the plate. Cook the kebabs for 5–6 minutes each side, until the meat is cooked through. Serve immediately with Lemon Pepper Pilaf (page 98).

Vietnamese Pork Sticks with Lettuce Wrap

Serves 4

500 g lean minced pork
6 tinned water chestnuts, finely chopped
1 clove garlic, finely chopped
1 green onion, finely chopped
1 tablespoon light soy sauce
2 teaspoons olive oil
1 teaspoon finely grated fresh ginger
¼ teaspoon caster sugar
¼ teaspoon chilli paste
1 teaspoon lime juice
12 wooden skewers (soaked in hot water for 20 minutes)
12 small cos lettuce leaves

夬 Mix together all the kebab ingredients in a bowl except the lettuce leaves. Using wet hands, form 12 sausage shapes from the mixture and carefully push a skewer through each one. Chill for 30 minutes.

夬 Preheat the barbecue to high and lightly oil the grill. Cook the kebabs for 3–4 minutes each side, until lightly browned all over and firm. Remove from the heat and slip the meat off the skewer into a lettuce leaf. Drizzle over Soy Ginger Dipping Sauce (page 127).

Chicken Kebabs with Tahini-style Sauce

Serves 4

> 3 single chicken breasts
> 2 garlic cloves, crushed
> 1 teaspoon grated lemon zest
> 2 teaspoons fresh lemon thyme leaves
> freshly ground black pepper
> ¼ cup olive oil
> 6 strips lemon peel
> 1 small red onion, peeled and cut into quarters
> 12 wooden skewers (soaked in hot water for 20 minutes)

丼 Cut the chicken breasts into bite-sized cubes. In a bowl, mix the chicken with the garlic, lemon zest, lemon thyme, pepper and oil. Marinate for 2 hours or longer in the fridge.

丼 Cut the strips of lemon peel into about 24 small pieces. Break the onion quarters apart into their layers. Skewer the chicken with alternate pieces of lemon peel and onion.

丼 Preheat the barbecue to medium–high and lightly oil the grill. Cook the kebabs for 4–6 minutes each side, until cooked through and lightly browned. Serve with Couscous Tabouli-style Salad (page 92) and Tahini-style Sauce (page 127).

Oriental Tuna Kebabs

Serves 4–6

600 g fresh tuna steaks
⅓ cup light soy sauce
⅓ cup mirin *or* dry sherry
1 teaspoon finely grated fresh ginger
1 clove garlic, crushed
1 teaspoon sesame oil
1 tablespoon light olive oil
pinch of salt and white pepper
3 Lebanese cucumbers, cut into cubes
12 wooden skewers (soaked in hot water for 20 minutes)

ㅈ Cut the tuna into bite-sized cubes. Mix together the soy sauce, mirin, ginger, garlic, oils and seasoning and pour over the tuna. Marinate for 1 hour in the fridge. Just before cooking, thread the tuna onto skewers with one or two pieces of cucumber.

ㅈ Preheat the barbecue to medium–high and lightly oil the grill. Cook the kebabs for 3–4 minutes each side. The tuna should be served rare to medium. Serve with crispy Asian Coleslaw (page 96).

Chilli Spiced Fish Kebab Sticks

Serves 4

400 g fresh tuna, redfish fillets, ling fillets *or* **swordfish**
1 tablespoon finely chopped fresh ginger
2 green onions, finely chopped
1 tablespoon finely chopped fresh chives
1 teaspoon chilli paste
1 tablespoon dry-roasted sesame seeds
1 tablespoon olive oil
16 wooden skewers (soaked in hot water for 20 minutes)
olive oil spray

⁊ Finely mince the fish in a food processor, then blend in the rest of the kebab ingredients. Shape the mixture into 16 sausages, keeping your hands moist to help with the shaping. Skewer each sausage and chill for 1 hour before cooking.

⁊ Preheat the barbecue to medium and lightly oil the plate or grill. Spray each kebab with a little oil and barbecue for 2–3 minutes each side. Serve immediately with sweet chilli sauce.

Spiced Prawn Kebabs

Serves 4

**24 green prawns, peeled and deveined but leaving the
heads on**
24 wooden skewers (soaked in hot water for 20 minutes)

Marinade
1 teaspoon Thai green curry paste
1 teaspoon brown sugar
1 teaspoon fish sauce
3 tablespoons lime juice
1 tablespoon peanut oil
2 tablespoons shredded kaffir lime leaves

஝ Mix all the marinade ingredients together and toss the prawns
through the mixture. Chill in the fridge for 1 hour, turning the prawns
occasionally.

஝ Preheat the barbecue to medium and lightly oil the grill. Thread a
skewer up through the tail of each prawn and out through the head. The
prawns should be straight on the skewer. Cook for 1–2 minutes each
side. Serve with Sweet and Sour Thai-style Relish (page 119) and plain
boiled rice.

Prawns and Pancetta Kebabs with Bay Leaves

Serves 4

> 16 large green prawns, peeled and deveined but leaving
>   the heads on
> 4 strips lemon peel
> 8 slices pancetta (hot *or* mild)
> 8 fresh bay leaves
> 8 wooden skewers (soaked in hot water for 20 minutes)

> Marinade
> ¼ cup light olive oil
> 1 tablespoon balsamic vinegar
> 1 tablespoon lemon juice
> 1 clove garlic, crushed
> 1 spring onion, finely chopped
> 1 crushed bay leaf

ㅈ Combine all the marinade ingredients and marinate the prawns for 30 minutes or longer (2 hours maximum).

ㅈ Cut each strip of lemon peel into two shorter pieces. Cut the slices of pancetta into two strips. Wrap a strip of pancetta around each prawn.

ㅈ Preheat the barbecue to medium and lightly oil the grill. Thread a pancetta-wrapped prawn onto a skewer, then a piece of lemon peel, then a second wrapped prawn, and finish up with a bay leaf on the end. Chill while the barbecue heats up. Brush the kebabs with the marinade and cook for 1–2 minutes each side. Serve with Sweet Red Onions with Raisins and Balsamic Vinegar (page 85) and Aïoli (page 118).

Scallop, Prosciutto and Water Chestnut Kebabs

Serves 4

**24 fresh white scallops, deveined and roe removed
   (about 250–300 g)**
16 tinned water chestnuts, drained
¼ cup light soy sauce
1 teaspoon freshly grated ginger
1 teaspoon white sugar
¼ teaspoon sesame oil
4 thin slices prosciutto
8 wooden skewers (soaked in hot water for 20 minutes)

丼 Place the scallops and water chestnuts in a bowl and mix in the soy sauce, ginger, sugar and sesame oil. Leave for 20 minutes to marinate. Cut the prosciutto into 16 pieces.

丼 Preheat the barbecue to medium high and lightly oil the grill. Thread each skewer with a scallop, a water chestnut, a piece of prosciutto, another scallop, another water chestnut, another piece of prosciutto and finally another scallop. Chill until ready to cook.

丼 Cook the kebabs for 3–4 minutes, turning a few times during the cooking. Serve with Asian Coleslaw (page 96).

Vegetable Kebabs with Parmesan Oil

Serves 4

3 medium-sized green zucchini, cut into chunks
2 medium-sized yellow zucchini *or* 8 yellow baby squash,
    cut into chunks
1 red pepper, deseeded and cut into chunks
1 green pepper, deseeded and cut into chunks
250 g yellow or red teardrop tomatoes *or* cherry tomatoes
1–2 tablespoons parmesan oil
salt and freshly ground black pepper
8 wooden skewers (soaked in hot water for 20 minutes)

⅄ Mix the vegetables together in a bowl with the parmesan oil.
Preheat the barbecue to high and lightly oil the grill.

⅄ Skewer the vegetables to make colourful rainbow kebabs. Cook the
kebabs for 3–4 minutes each side, until lightly browned. Serve with Basil
Pesto (page 117).

Vegetables

Marinated Summer Vegetables

Serves 4-6

> 1 red pepper, deseeded and cut into quarters
> 1 green pepper, deseeded and cut into quarters
> 4 large zucchini, sliced in half lengthways
> 1 eggplant, cut into thick rounds
> 4 red onions, peeled and cut into quarters
> 250 g fresh baby corn
> ½ cup stoned and roughly chopped kalamata olives

> Marinade
> 1 cup olive oil
> 1 tablespoon finely chopped flat-leaf parsley
> 1 tablespoon finely chopped fresh basil
> 2 cloves garlic, finely chopped
> salt and freshly ground black pepper

৯ Mix together the marinade ingredients in a baking dish and add the vegetables. Set aside for 1 hour.

৯ Preheat the barbecue to medium-high and lightly oil the grill. Drain the vegetables from the marinade and cook for 4-5 minutes or until tender, turning once. Arrange on a serving platter and scatter over the olives.

Variations

Use other vegetables when in season, such as fennel, asparagus, endive, yellow squash, green onions or mushrooms.

Chargrilled Red Peppers with Tomatoes and Feta

Serves 4

250 g cherry tomatoes, cut in half
1 cup chopped creamy feta
½ cup chopped flat-leaf parsley
2 cloves garlic, finely chopped
3 tablespoons virgin olive oil
4 red *or* yellow peppers, cut in half, seeds and membranes
    removed
salt and freshly ground black pepper
extra-virgin olive oil, for drizzling

A Mix the tomatoes with the feta, parsley, garlic and 1 tablespoon of the olive oil. Brush the remaining 2 tablespoons of oil over the pepper halves and season with salt and pepper.

A Preheat the barbecue to medium and lightly oil the grill. Cook the peppers, cut-side down for 4 minutes. Turn and spoon the tomato mixture into the halves. Cook for 6 minutes, or until the peppers have softened and the feta has melted a little. Remove and serve immediately, drizzled with a little extra-virgin olive oil. This is delicious served hot or cold.

Barbecued Potatoes with Rosemary and Garlic

Serves 4

400 g new potatoes
4 cloves garlic, smashed
4 sprigs rosemary
4 tablespoons light olive oil

⊼ Preheat the barbecue to medium–high. Prepare four sheets of double-thickness foil. Distribute the potatoes evenly between the four sheets, dotting with garlic, rosemary and olive oil. Seal each parcel.

⊼ Cook for 15–20 minutes, or until tender.

Spicy Potato Wedges

Serves 4

400 g potatoes
2–3 tablespoons olive oil
1 teaspoon medium-heat chilli powder
2 teaspoons ground cumin
2 teaspoons ground sweet paprika
1 teaspoon ground oregano leaves
¼ teaspoon salt

卅 Cut the potatoes into even, thin wedges. Mix the oil and spices together and rub all over the potatoes. Preheat the barbecue to high and lightly oil the grill.

卅 Cook the potatoes, cut-side down, for about 6–8 minutes. Turn the heat down and cook for 12 minutes, turning a couple of times. Remove the potatoes and cover tightly with foil for 5 minutes. This will help steam the potatoes and cook them through. Serve immediately with Aïoli (page 118).

Sweet Potato with Honey and Soy Glaze

Serves 4

400 g sweet potatoes, washed and scrubbed
2 tablespoons honey
2 tablespoons light soy sauce
1 teaspoon freshly grated ginger
2 tablespoons light olive oil

៱ Cut the sweet potatoes into thin (1 cm thick) slices. Mix together the honey, soy sauce, ginger and oil and coat the slices.

៱ Preheat the barbecue to medium and lightly oil the grill. Cook the sweet potato slices for 2–3 minutes each side, until softened. Remove and cover with foil for 2–3 minutes to finish cooking. Serve with grilled meats or fish.

Variation

You can use a mixture of pumpkin and sweet potato, if you like.

Sweet Red Onions with Raisins and Balsamic Vinegar

Serves 4

¼ cup raisins
1 tablespoon balsamic vinegar
1 tablespoon olive oil
salt and freshly ground black pepper
4 medium red onions, peeled and halved lengthways

茶 Mix the raisins with the balsamic vinegar and oil, and season with salt and pepper. Prepare four sheets of double-thickness foil. Place half an onion on each sheet and sprinkle over a few marinated raisins. Top with the other onion half and wrap securely in foil.

茶 Preheat the barbecue grill to medium. Cook the onion parcels for 30 minutes or until the onions are tender, turning a couple of times during the cooking. Remove from the heat and rest for 2–3 minutes. Serve with grilled meats or chicken.

Orange-glazed Beetroot
with Rosemary

Serves 4

½ cup fresh orange juice
2 tablespoons honey
1 teaspoon dried rosemary leaves
2 tablespoons olive oil
4 medium-sized whole beetroots, peeled and stalks
 trimmed

ಸ Preheat the barbecue to medium.

ಸ Mix the orange juice, honey, rosemary and oil together. Prepare
four sheets of double-thickness foil. Cut a cross shape on the top of
each beetroot and place a beetroot on each sheet of foil. Gather the foil
around to make a parcel, then pour a little of the marinade into each
parcel. Seal the top.

ಸ Cook the beetroot parcels for 30–40 minutes, turning frequently,
until the beetroot is tender. Serve with grilled lamb or beef or Lemon
Pepper Pilaf (page 98).

Grilled Corn on the Husk with Herbed Butter

Serves 4

4 cobs corn, with husks
½ cup Herbed Butter (page 128)

⅄ Preheat the barbecue to medium and lightly oil the grill.

⅄ Soak the corn husks in a bowl of water for 10 minutes. Remove from the water and drain. Carefully peel back the ears of corn and remove the silk threads. Spread a little herbed butter along the corn and press back the ears. Tie with kitchen string to secure at the top.

⅄ Cook for 20–30 minutes, turning frequently.

Field Mushrooms with Pesto

Serves 4

> 8 large, flat field mushrooms
> ½ cup fresh lemon juice
> 3 tablespoons light olive oil
> 2 cloves garlic, finely chopped
> salt and freshly ground black pepper
> ¼ cup Basil Pesto (page 117)

barbecue Preheat the barbecue to medium and lightly oil the grill. Wipe the mushrooms with a damp cloth and trim the stems. Whisk the lemon juice, oil, garlic and seasoning together in a bowl. Brush all over the mushrooms to coat.

barbecue Cook for 2 minutes, cup-side down, then turn and cook for 2–3 minutes on the other side. When the mushrooms start to soften, remove and spoon a little pesto into the cup. Serve immediately.

Teriyaki Eggplant Slices with Toasted Sesame Seeds

Serves 4

4–6 Japanese eggplants, sliced lengthways
4 tablespoons sesame seeds

Marinade
3 tablespoons light soy sauce
3 tablespoon mirin *or* sake (Japanese rice vinegar)
2 teaspoons sesame oil
1 teaspoon grated fresh ginger
1 tablespoon brown sugar

尺 Mix together the marinade ingredients and use the mixture to coat the eggplant on both sides. Set aside.

尺 Preheat the barbecue to high and lightly oil the grill. Toast the sesame seeds by heating a small saucepan over medium heat. Add the sesame seeds and toss for 2–3 minutes, until the seeds are lightly browned. Remove immediately from the heat.

尺 Cook the eggplant slices for 3–4 minutes each side, brushing with a little marinade before they are turned. Remove from the heat. Toss over the sesame seeds and serve immediately. This makes a delicious salad and can be mixed through watercress leaves or baby rocket.

Spicy Asparagus Spears with Creamy Sweet Chilli Dip

Serves 4

¼ cup olive oil
2 cloves garlic, finely chopped
½ teaspoon chilli paste
24 fresh asparagus spears, bases trimmed
2 tablespoons sweet chilli sauce
½ cup sour cream
1 tablespoon finely chopped fresh mint

☗ Preheat the barbecue to medium–high.

☗ Mix together the oil, garlic and chilli paste and brush over the asparagus spears. Cook the asparagus for 3–4 minutes, turning frequently until they are just tender. Meanwhile, mix the sweet chilli sauce, sour cream and fresh mint until well combined. Remove the asparagus from the heat and serve on a platter with the dipping sauce.

Salads and
Accompaniments

Couscous Tabouli-style Salad

Serves 4

1 cup instant couscous
1 cup boiling water
1 eggplant, cut into rounds, then each round cut in half
250 g cherry tomatoes
2 Lebanese cucumbers roughly chopped
6 green onions, finely chopped
1 bunch flat-leaf parsley

Dressing
¼ cup olive oil
¼ cup freshly squeezed lemon juice
1 teaspoon Dijon mustard

ⴲ Mix the couscous with the boiling water and allow to stand, covered, for 5 minutes. Use a fork to separate the grains.

ⴲ Preheat the barbecue to medium and lightly oil the grill. Cook the eggplant for 2–3 minutes each side.

ⴲ Mix together the dressing ingredients in a large bowl and toss in the eggplant, cherry tomato, cucumber and green onion. Stir in the couscous and parsley, and serve.

Greek-style Salad

Serves 4

4 roma tomatoes, roughly chopped
2 Lebanese cucumbers, halved and seeds removed,
   roughly chopped
150 g feta, cut into small cubes
1 red onion, thinly sliced
½ cup stoned kalamata olives
3 tablespoons extra-virgin olive oil
juice of 1 lemon
pinch of salt
cracked black pepper
2 cups baby rocket

Mix together the tomato, cucumber, feta, onion, olives, olive oil and lemon juice in a large bowl. Season to taste with salt and pepper. Mix in the baby rocket and mound onto a serving plate. Serve immediately.

Savoury Mango and Pear Salad

Serves 4

juice and finely grated zest of 1 lime
1 tablespoon sugar
1 tablespoon fish sauce
2 tablespoons finely chopped fresh mint
1 tablespoon finely chopped fresh coriander
1 carrot, peeled and grated
2 nashi pears, peeled, cored and grated
1 small cantaloupe (rockmelon), peeled and julienned
1 large, firm mango, peeled, halved and julienned

⩗ Mix together the lime juice, zest, sugar, fish sauce and herbs and gently stir in the carrot and fruit. Chill for 30 minutes before serving.

Variation

If green pawpaws or green mangoes are in season, use them instead of the nashi pears or mango.

Roasted Beetroot Salad with Orange Dressing

Serves 4

3 medium beetroots, stalks removed

Dressing
¼ cup fresh orange juice
1 teaspoon honey
1 teaspoon balsamic vinegar
1 teaspoon Dijon mustard
1 tablespoon extra-virgin olive oil
salt and freshly ground black pepper
4 cups mixed lettuce leaves, washed and spun dry

⛩ Preheat the barbecue to high. Cut the beetroots into four and wrap each one in double-thickness foil. Cook for about 20–25 minutes, until the beetroot is tender. Remove and cool a little.

⛩ Mix together the dressing ingredients. Peel the beetroot and cut into thick chunks. Mix into the dressing, then add to a salad bowl filled with the lettuce leaves and toss well. Serve immediately.

Asian Coleslaw

Serves 4–6

¼ cup sesame seeds
¼ green cabbage, cored and finely shredded
1 cup beansprouts, rinsed and drained
1 red pepper, deseeded and thinly sliced
2 carrots, peeled and coarsely grated
1 small red onion, very thinly sliced

Dressing
2 tablespoons brown sugar
1 tablespoon smooth peanut butter
1 tablespoon sesame oil
2 tablespoons light olive oil
3 tablespoons lime juice
1 fresh chilli, deseeded and finely chopped (optional)

只 Heat a small saucepan over medium heat. Add the sesame seeds
and toss for 2–3 minutes, until the seeds are lightly browned. Remove
immediately from the heat.

只 Mix together all the salad ingredients except the sesame seeds.
For the dressing, whisk together all the ingredients. Pour over the salad
and toss to coat, then sprinkle over the sesame seeds. Cover until ready
to serve.

Hokkien Noodles with Mushrooms and Chinese Cabbage

Serves 4

1 teaspoon sesame seeds
1 tablespoon light olive oil
¼ Chinese cabbage, finely shredded
100 g mushrooms, thinly sliced
400 g Hokkien noodles, soaked in boiling water for
    5 minutes, then drained
2 tablespoons soy sauce
1 teaspoon sesame oil

A Heat a small saucepan over medium heat. Add the sesame seeds and toss for 2–3 minutes, until the seeds are lightly browned. Remove immediately from the heat.

A Heat a frying pan or wok and add the oil. Stir-fry the cabbage and mushrooms for 3–4 minutes, until just beginning to wilt. Stir in the noodles, soy sauce, sesame oil and toasted sesame seeds. Stir-fry for 3 minutes, until well combined. Serve immediately.

Lemon Pepper Pilaf

Serves 4

> 2 tablespoons olive oil
> 1 small onion, finely chopped
> 1 clove garlic, finely chopped
> 1 cup long-grain rice
> 1 teaspoon finely grated lemon zest
> 2 cups chicken stock
> ½ teaspoon freshly ground black pepper
> pinch of salt
> 1 tablespoon finely chopped fresh parsley

茶 Heat the oil in a saucepan and cook the onion and garlic over low heat for 2–3 minutes, until softened. Stir in the rice and lemon zest and cook for 2 minutes. Slowly pour in the stock and bring to the boil. Cover the pan and simmer for 20 minutes, or until all the liquid is absorbed. Remove from the heat and remove the lid. Season with salt and pepper and stir in the parsley. Serve immediately.

Zucchini Fritters

Makes 8

2 large zucchini (about 500 g), coarsely grated
1 teaspoon salt
1 tablespoon freshly grated lemon zest
1 tablespoon finely chopped flat-leaf parsley
1 clove garlic, finely chopped
freshly ground black pepper
2 eggs, lightly beaten
½ cup plain flour
2–3 tablespoons light olive oil

禾 Combine the zucchini, salt, lemon zest, parsley, garlic and pepper in a mixing bowl. Stir in the egg and the flour, making sure there are no lumps left in the mixture.

禾 Heat the oil in a large, non-stick frying pan over medium heat. Drop about 3 tablespoons of the mixture into the pan and cook for 2–3 minutes, until golden brown. Turn the heat down a little and flip the fritter to cook the other side for 2–3 minutes. Remove and drain on kitchen paper. Keep warm while you cook the remaining fritters. Add a little more oil to the pan if necessary. Serve with lemon wedges and grilled fish or chicken.

Potato Pancakes

Makes 8

2 medium-sized floury potatoes, peeled and grated
2 green onions, finely chopped
2 tablespoons self-raising flour
1 egg, lightly beaten
1 tablespoon finely chopped fresh chives
pinch of salt and freshly ground black pepper
2 tablespoons olive oil

҂ Place the grated potato in a sieve and squeeze out as much moisture as possible over a mixing bowl. In a separate bowl mix the green onion, flour, egg, chives and seasoning. Stir in the drained potato and mix well.

҂ Preheat the barbecue to medium and generously oil the plate. (You can use a frying pan if you prefer.) Drop heaped tablespoons of the potato mixture onto the plate. Flatten with a spatula. Cook until lightly browned on the bottom, then turn to brown the other side – about 3–4 minutes each side. Keep pancakes warm in the oven until ready to serve.

Orzo with Fresh Parmesan and Basil

Serves 4

25 g butter
1½ cups orzo (small rice-shaped pasta)
3 cups chicken *or* vegetable stock
¼ cup freshly grated parmesan
¼ cup roughly chopped fresh basil
salt and freshly ground black pepper

祭 Melt the butter in a heavy saucepan over medium heat. Stir in the orzo and cook for 2–3 minutes. Add the stock and bring to the boil. Cover and turn the heat to very low. Cook for about 20 minutes, until the liquid has been absorbed and the orzo is tender. Stir in the parmesan and basil, season to taste and serve immediately with grilled seafood or chicken or pork.

White Bean Purée

Serves 4–6

2 × 425 g tins cannellini beans, drained
1 teaspoon ground cumin
2 tablespoons lemon juice
3–4 tablespoons olive oil
1 tablespoon finely chopped fresh parsley

⊼ Blend all the ingredients in a food processor. Serve the purée at room temperature as an accompaniment, much like potatoes or rice.

Minted Broad Bean Purée

Serves 4–6

500 g freshly shelled *or* frozen broad beans
1 teaspoon lemon juice
2–3 tablespoons crème fraîche
1 tablespoon finely chopped fresh mint

Cook the broad beans in boiling water for 6–8 minutes, until tender. Drain and refresh under cold running water, removing the skins. In a food processor blend the beans with the lemon juice. Remove and stir in the crème fraîche and mint. Serve at room temperature.

Desserts

Chargrilled Peaches with Ricotta and Amaretti Cream

Serves 4

4 firm slipstone peaches, cut in half and stones removed
¼ cup melted butter

Ricotta and Amaretti Cream
1 cup fresh ricotta
¼ cup whipping cream
1 tablespoon caster sugar
6 amaretti biscuits, crushed
1 teaspoon marsala

⊼ To make the ricotta and amaretti cream, blend the ricotta in a food processor with the cream and sugar for 2–3 minutes, until smooth. Remove and stir through the crushed amaretti biscuits and marsala. Chill until ready to serve.

⊼ Preheat the barbecue to medium and lightly oil the plate or grill. Brush the cut side of each peach half with butter and cook for 3–4 minutes. Turn and cook for a further 2–3 minutes. Serve with ricotta and amaretti cream.

Rum-spiced Summer Fruits

Serves 4

4 fresh firm figs
4 fresh small nectarines
4 fresh small peaches
4 fresh apricots
½ cup lemon juice
4 tablespoons brown sugar
1 tablespoon dark rum
½ teaspoon ground cinnamon

Cut the fruit in half, removing any stones. Mix together the lemon juice, brown sugar, rum and cinnamon and toss the fruit in this mixture.

Preheat the barbecue to medium and lightly oil the plate. Cook the fruit for 2–4 minutes each side, until soft and lightly browned. Serve with ice-cream or cream.

Grilled Mango Cheeks with Honey and Cardamom

Serves 4

4 large mangoes, cheeks removed
½ cup honey
½ teaspoon ground cardamom
¼ cup lime juice

Ṝ Preheat the barbecue to medium and lightly oil the plate.

Ṝ With a sharp knife, score the mango cheeks in a diamond pattern. Mix together the honey, cardamom and lime juice and brush over the cut side of each mango cheek. Cook, cut-side down, for 3 minutes, or until lightly browned. Remove and serve with vanilla yoghurt or ice-cream.

Spicy Rum Bananas

Serves 4

> **4 large, ripe, firm bananas**
> **1 tablespoon butter, melted**
> **1 tablespoon dark rum**
> **¼ teaspoon ground mixed spice**
> **½ tablespoon soft brown sugar**

🐾 Remove the skin and a thin strip of fruit from one side of each banana with a sharp knife. Mix together the melted butter, rum, mixed spice and sugar and brush over the cut side of the banana. Reserve the remaining mixture.

🐾 Preheat the barbecue to medium and lightly oil the plate or grill. Grill the bananas, skin-side down, until blackened. Remove and spoon the rum mixture over the warm bananas. Serve with ice-cream or whipped cream.

Grilled Pineapple Wedges with Lime and Golden Syrup

Serves 4

¼ cup lime juice
2 tablespoons golden syrup
1 small pineapple

朲 Mix together the lime juice and golden syrup. Carefully remove the skin from the pineapple, then cut the pineapple into four lengthways and remove the core.

朲 Preheat the barbecue to medium and lightly oil the grill. Brush the marinade over the pineapple and cook until lightly charred all over. Remove and serve with vanilla ice-cream or Chocolate Fudge Sauce (page 130).

Banana and Pineapple Kebabs with Yoghurt and Honey Cream

Serves 4

2 bananas
a squeeze of lemon juice
¼ cup melted butter
1 tablespoon brown sugar
1 tablespoon dark rum
pinch of ground cardamom
½ pineapple, peeled, cored and cubed
8 wooden skewers (soaked in hot water for 20 minutes)

Yoghurt and Honey Cream
1 cup whipping cream
½ cup creamy plain yoghurt
2 tablespoons honey

鼎 To make the yoghurt and honey cream, beat the cream until thick, then fold through the yoghurt and honey. Set aside and chill until ready to serve.

鼎 Cut the bananas into large chunks and place in a mixing bowl with a little lemon juice. In a separate bowl, mix together the butter, sugar, rum and cardamom.

鼎 Thread the pineapple cubes onto the skewers, alternating with banana chunks, and brush with the butter mixture. Preheat the barbecue to medium and lightly oil the grill. Cook the kebabs for 2–3 minutes each side, brushing once with the marinade. Remove and serve with the yoghurt and honey cream.

Stuffed Apples with Craisins and Brown Sugar

Serves 4

4 small Granny Smith apples
4 tablespoons craisins (dried and sweetened cranberries)
20 g softened butter
2 tablespoons soft brown sugar

卄 Core the apples and slice from top to bottom, but not quite all the way through. Mix together the craisins, butter and sugar and stuff into the cavity.

卄 Preheat the barbecue to medium. Wrap each apple in a double thickness of foil. Cook for 30 minutes, or until the apples are soft. Serve hot with ice-cream or custard.

Grilled Pears with Vanilla Sugar

Serves 4

4 medium-sized, ripe, firm pears, peeled, halved and cored
3 teaspoons vanilla essence
2 tablespoons caster sugar
20 g softened butter

𝕉 With a sharp knife, score the round side of each pear half several times. Mix together the vanilla essence, sugar and butter. Place two half pears flat-side down on a sheet of double-thickness foil. Place a knob of butter on top of each one and wrap the foil around to seal. Wrap the remaining pears in the same way. Set aside while you prepare the barbecue.

𝕉 Preheat the barbecue to medium. Cook the foil-wrapped pears for 20 minutes. Remove the pears from the foil, reserving the juices, and place scored-side down on the grill. Cook for 5 minutes, until lightly brown. Remove and serve with the pear syrup and whipped cream or custard.

Sauces

Spicy Coriander Pesto

Makes 1 cup

1 cup roasted cashew nuts
2 handfuls coriander, washed and roots stripped
2 green chillies
juice of 1 lemon
1 teaspoon finely grated lemon zest
1 teaspoon fish sauce
½ cup light olive oil *or* peanut oil
a little olive *or* peanut oil, extra

弄 Place all the ingredients except the extra oil in a food processor and blend to a smooth paste. Remove to an airtight container and pour the extra oil over the top. Seal and store until ready to use. The pesto keeps for 3–5 days in the fridge.

Basil Pesto

Makes 1 cup

2 cups fresh basil leaves
60 g parmesan, in small chunks
60 g pine nuts
2 cloves garlic, crushed
100 ml olive oil
a little olive oil, extra

⍟ Place all the ingredients except the oil in a food processor and blend to a paste. With the motor running, slowly pour in the oil until it combines to make a creamy sauce. Remove to an airtight container and pour the extra oil over the top. Seal and store until ready to use. The pesto keeps for 3–5 days in the fridge.

Variations

Instead of basil, use 2 cups of baby rocket, baby spinach, coriander or parsley. Instead of pine nuts, use blanched almonds, roasted cashew nuts (good with coriander), roasted peanuts (also good with coriander) or walnuts (good with parsley). Experiment with flavours by adding a little orange, lime or lemon zest, ground black pepper or chilli paste.

Aïoli

Makes about 1¼ cups

> **6 cloves garlic, crushed**
> **½ teaspoon salt**
> **2 egg yolks**
> **1 cup olive oil**
> **2 teaspoons lemon juice**
> **pinch of white pepper**

⧆ In a food processor or mortar and pestle, blend or pound the garlic with the salt until finely crushed. Add the egg yolks and mix well. Slowly pour in the olive oil and blend to form a thick mayonnaise. Season with lemon juice and white pepper. The Aïoli keeps for up to 5 days, in an airtight container, in the refrigerator.

Sweet and Sour Thai-style Relish

Makes 2 cups

1 cup white vinegar
1 cup caster sugar
½ teaspoon salt
1 telegraph cucumber, halved and deseeded
1 small carrot, peeled and finely chopped
2 small red chillies, deseeded
⅓ cup roasted peanuts, roughly chopped
1 handful fresh coriander, finely chopped

⋔ Put the vinegar, sugar and salt in a small saucepan and slowly bring to the boil over gentle heat. Boil for 2 minutes, stirring occasionally. Remove from the heat and cool. Pour into a mixing bowl.

⋔ Finely chop the cucumber and stir into the vinegar syrup. Add the carrot, chilli, peanuts and coriander. Stir well to combine. Refrigerate until ready to serve. The relish keeps for 2 days, covered, in the refrigerator.

Roasted Tomato Relish

Makes about 1 cup

250 g ripe tomatoes, halved
1 red pepper, cut into quarters and deseeded
1 red onion, finely chopped
2 cloves garlic, crushed
3 tablespoons olive oil
salt and freshly ground black pepper
1 tablespoon balsamic vinegar

⧉ Preheat the oven to 180°C. Place the tomato, capsicum, onion and garlic in a roasting pan and bake for 30 minutes, until the vegetables are soft. Remove and cool. Roughly chop in a food processor or by hand. Season to taste and add the balsamic vinegar. Refrigerate until ready to use. The relish keeps for up to 4 days, in an airtight container, in the refrigerator.

Variation

Spicy Tomato Relish
Add 1–2 teaspoons of Harissa (page 126) to the cooled tomato relish.

Mayonnaise

Makes about 1½ cups

>2 large egg yolks
>1 teaspoon lemon juice *or* white wine vinegar
>½ teaspoon Dijon mustard
>1 cup vegetable *or* olive oil
>salt and freshly ground black pepper

⊼ Place the egg yolks, lemon juice and mustard in a small bowl and, using a small balloon whisk, whisk for 1–2 minutes. Slowly drizzle the oil in, whisking vigorously until the oil starts to emulsify with the egg yolks. Keep whisking until all the oil is incorporated and the mayonnaise is thick and creamy. Season with salt and pepper. The mayonnaise will keep for 8–10 days in the fridge.

–< **Tip: This recipe can also be made in a food processor or blender, but it will not be as thick as the hand-whisked sauce.**

–< **Tip: If the mayonnaise separates, place two more egg yolks in a separate bowl and slowly whisk into the curdled sauce. Add a little more oil once the mixture has thickened, and a teaspoon of lemon juice and mustard for extra flavour.**

Variations

Try adding ½ a teaspoon of wasabi for Wasabi Mayonnaise; ¼ cup of finely chopped mint and coriander for Mint and Coriander Mayonnaise; and ¼ of a cup of coarse-grain mustard and 1 tablespoon of finely chopped fresh parsley for Mustard Mayonnaise.

Hollandaise Sauce

Makes about 1 cup

4 egg yolks
1 tablespoon cold water
200 g softened butter
pinch of salt and white pepper
1–2 tablespoons lemon juice *or* **white wine vinegar**

禾 In a bowl, beat the eggs and water with a whisk until light and fluffy. Pour into a bowl set over a saucepan of barely simmering water. Stir for 2–3 minutes, until warm. Whisk in the butter, about 2 tablespoons at a time, until each quantity is emulsified into the eggs. When all the butter is combined, whisk for 2–3 minutes until the sauce is thick enough to coat the back of a wooden spoon. Whisk in the seasoning and lemon juice or vinegar. Set aside until ready to use.

禾 Do not refrigerate. This sauce should always be served warm. The sauce will solidify if made ahead of serving time. To re-heat, place over a pan of hot water and whisk until the sauce is warm. Serve immediately.

Béarnaise Sauce

Makes about 1¼ cups

¼ cup white wine
¼ cup white wine vinegar
1 teaspoon dried tarragon
1 tablespoons finely chopped green onion
pinch of salt and freshly ground black pepper

⌂ Combine all the ingredients in a small saucepan and bring to the boil. Simmer until the mixture has reduced by half. Rapidly boil again to reduce by another half, leaving about 2 tablespoons of liquid. Strain into a bowl.

⌂ Make a hollandaise sauce (see opposite) but whisk in the reduced vinegar mixture instead of the lemon juice. Serve immediately or at room temperature.

⌐ **Tip: If the sauce curdles, vigorously whisk 2 tablespoons of hot water into the mixture, or place the bowl over ice to stop the cooking and then whisk until smooth.**

Dill Mustard Sauce

Makes about 1 cup

¼ cup chopped dill
1 teaspoon dried English mustard
3 tablespoons white wine vinegar
1 cup olive oil

冗 In a food processor blend the dill, mustard and white wine vinegar, then slowly drizzle in the oil to combine. The sauce keeps for 5 days, in an airtight container, in the refrigerator.

Fresh Mint Sauce

Makes about 1½ cups

1 cup white wine vinegar
1 cup caster sugar
1 cup finely chopped fresh mint

⊼ Stir the vinegar and sugar together in a bowl until the sugar has dissolved. Add the mint and stir into the vinegar mixture. Store in an airtight container in the fridge until ready to use. The sauce keeps for 2 weeks.

Harissa

Makes about 1 cup

**30 g dried chillies, stalks removed (*or* 60 g fresh red
chillies)**
6 cloves garlic, crushed
1 teaspoon salt
1 handful coriander leaves and stalks
½ cup mint leaves
¼ cup olive oil

斉 Soak the dried chillies in hot water for 10 minutes to soften them.
Drain and place into a food processor along with the garlic, salt,
coriander and mint. Process for 3–4 minutes, then slowly add the oil.
Remove and store in an airtight container in the fridge until ready to use.
Keeps for 3 weeks.

Tahini-style Sauce

Makes about 1 cup

> **juice of 1 lemon**
> **½ cup tahini paste**
> **1 teaspoon dry-roasted cumin seeds**
> **2 tablespoons freshly chopped flat-leaf parsley**
> **salt and freshly ground black pepper**

Place all the ingredients in a food processor and blend to combine. Slowly add 3–5 tablespoons of water to mix to a thin dipping sauce. Keeps for 2 weeks, in an airtight container, in the refrigerator.

Soy Ginger Dipping Sauce

Makes about ½ cup

> **3 tablespoons mirin or dry sherry**
> **1 teaspoon freshly grated ginger**
> **3 tablespoons light soy sauce**
> **1 teaspoon sugar**

Combine all ingredients. The sauce will keep for 5 days, in an airtight container, in the refrigerator.

Dill Butter

125 g very soft unsalted butter
3–4 tablespoons finely chopped fresh dill
pinch of freshly grated nutmeg

兀 Mash all the ingredients together with a fork or in a food processor,
until well combined. Wrap in non-stick baking paper or foil and shape
into a log. Chill until ready to use. To serve, cut into small rounds and
melt over grilled meat or vegetables.

Variations

Use the method above to make flavoured butters of your choice.

Garlic Butter
125 g very soft unsalted butter
2 cloves garlic, finely minced
pinch of salt and freshly ground pepper

Mustard Butter
125 g very soft unsalted butter
2 tablespoons coarse-grain mustard
pinch of salt and freshly ground pepper

Herbed Butter
125 g very soft unsalted butter
3–4 tablespoons finely chopped fresh herbs (parsley,
mint and coriander)

Flavoured Oils

several large pieces of bruised fresh lemon peel
large sprig of fresh rosemary *or* **thyme and 6 peppercorns**
2 small, fresh, bruised chillies
1–2 small chunks of best-quality parmesan

卍 Add any of the above to 400 ml good-quality virgin olive oil *or* light olive oil *or* vegetable oil and leave to stand in a cool, dark place for at least 1 week before using. Oils give moisture and flavour to cooking and enhance the simplest barbecued meat, seafood or vegetable.

Chocolate Fudge Sauce

Makes about 1½ cups

100 ml cream
25 g cocoa powder
100 g caster sugar
½ cup golden syrup
25 g butter
pinch of salt
½ teaspoon vanilla essence

ᚱ Mix together all the ingredients except the vanilla essence in a saucepan over low heat. Slowly bring to the boil and simmer, stirring occasionally, for 4–5 minutes. Stir in the vanilla essence. Remove from the heat and cool a little before serving with grilled fruit desserts. Keeps for 4 days, in an airtight container in the refrigerator. Warm sauce before serving.

Pink Sabayon Sauce

Makes about 1 cup

4 egg yolks
75 g caster sugar
200 ml pink sparkling wine
1 teaspoon vanilla essence

〒 In a mixing bowl over a pan of simmering water, whisk the egg yolks, sugar, wine and vanilla essence with a balloon whisk until thick and creamy. Serve immediately with hot grilled fruit.

Sweet Rum Butter

Makes about 1 cup

> **100 g very soft unsalted butter**
> **100 g sifted icing sugar**
> **1½ tablespoons rum *or* brandy**

 Blend together all the ingredients in a food processor, or by hand with a fork. Wrap in non-stick baking paper or foil and shape into a log. Chill until ready to use. To serve, cut into small rounds and melt over hot grilled fruit.

Index